THE UGLY SPIRIT

Russell Barr

THE UGLY SPIRIT

OBERON BOOKS
LONDON

First published in 2012 by Oberon Books Ltd
521 Caledonian Road, London N7 9RH
Tel: +44 (0) 20 7607 3637 / Fax: +44 (0) 20 7607 3629
e-mail: info@oberonbooks.com

A catalogue record for this book is available from the British Library.

PB ISBN: 978-1-84943-222-1
Digital ISBN: 978-1-84943-536-9

Cover image by Charles McQuillan/Pacemaker Press.

This play is dedicated to two great friends,
who are no longer with us.

James Lynch, the kindest man I ever met,
and to Katie, my remarkable Jack Russell Terrier.

James and Katie were a shining example of how to live and love.

Let their way, be our way.

The writer would also like to thank
the following for their continued support:

Sally and Graham Crowley, Ruth Young, St John Donald, Rachel
Hopkins, Jess Alford, Natasha Davis, Lisa Williamson, Joanna
Scanlan, Alan Rickman, Yve Newbold, Auntie Sheila Livingstone,
Garry Robson, Deborah Wintle and everybody at Fittings
Multimedia Arts, and the Cultural Olympiad.

The writer would especially like to thank his family, Mum, Dad,
Julie, Alison, Scott, Danny, Evie, Andrew and Wee Findlay,
without them, he would never have come this far.

A small but sweet thank you goes to the writer's terrier,
Mr H. Pocket.

The Ugly Spirit is an Unlimited Commission for the Cultural Olympiad. First performed on the 19 May 2012 with the following cast:

In Order of Appearance:

THE SPECIAL DETACHMENT	David Hoyle
LADY SCHWARZKOPF	Denise Leigh
JESSIE	Gareth Kieran Jones
BESSIE	Rachel Drazek
TRAIN DRIVER	A Rat

Creative Team

Director: Garry Robson

Musical Director: Stefan Andrusyschyn

Writer: Russell Barr

Associate Artist: Tanya Raabe

Designer: Lisa Ducie

Lighting Design: Ian Scott

Artistic Consultant: Peter Higgin

Unlimited encourages collaborations and partnerships between disability arts organisations, disabled and deaf artists, producers and mainstream organisations to celebrate the inspiration of the Olympic and Paralympic Games and to create original and exciting works. Twenty-nine Unlimited Commissions have been awarded.

Unlimited is principally funded by the National Lottery through the Olympic Lottery Distributor and is delivered in partnership with London 2012, Arts Council England, Creative Scotland, Arts Council of Wales, Arts Council of Northern Ireland and the British Council.

The Ugly Spirit was originally commissioned and first performed by Fittings Multimedia Arts. As part of the creative development of the work Fittings staged a series of workshops, development weeks and events.

As part of this process we would like to acknowledge the involvement and participation of the following groups:

Homotopia, Liverpool
Hereward College, Coventry
Contact the Elderly, London
Project Ability, Glasgow
DaDaFest International 2010

and performers:
David Hoyle
Robert Softley
Sally Clay
Kiruna Stamell
Eileen Nicholas

Fittings Multimedia Arts is a disability led NPO with offices in Liverpool and Scotland.

We have been developing mixed media projects since 1995.

All our work is created through New Writing and made with artists and performers from different cultures and life experiences.

We fuse various styles of performance and storytelling to produce new works that address serious issues in the language of variety theatre.

We make shows that are accessible and relevant to audiences from diverse communities, ages and educational backgrounds. Our work is exciting, visceral and entertaining, presented in a variety of settings and media and accompanied by extensive workshop and outreach programmes.

www.fittings.org.uk

Characters

(in order of appearance)

THE SPECIAL DETACHMENT
a Nazi who hates uniforms

LADY SCHWARZKOPF
an Opera Singer with Nazi tendencies

JESSIE
a Jew

BESSIE
a Jew

TRAIN DRIVER
who can either be played by a live gerbil,
hamster, rat, or any other suitable rodent.

When the symbol '/' appears, it denotes when
the next person should start speaking.

Berlin. 1973. A bombed ballroom. There has been a children's Birthday Party. The party was many years ago.

There are thirteen 1940s children's chairs.

There is a large pile of stones. They have been carefully placed.

There are two brown linen bags filled with stones beside each of the twins.

Above the stage, there is a model train track. The train is driven by a live rodent.

LADY SCHWARZKOPF, an opera singer is lying face down on an army blanket. She is wearing a white linen night dress, which has blood splattered across the back. She has bare feet.

JESSIE and BESSIE. Twins. They are joined by the ribcage. It is clear that they have been sewn together. BESSIE and JESSIE are wearing 1940s children's clothes. The clothes are ill-fitting, worn and dirty. They are both asleep. JESSIE is clutching an unopened present which is wrapped in 1940s wrapping paper. JESSIE has a pair of binoculars hung round his neck.

The stage gradually fills with fog.

LADY SCHWARZKOPF stands.

THE SPECIAL DETACHMENT enters on to the stage with the audience, he is wearing a non-specific uniform. THE SPECIAL DETACHMENT is feeding the audience strawberries.

The audience are faced with themselves.

LADY SCHWARZKOPF stands.

There is a loud explosion.

The stage goes dark.

THE SPECIAL DETACHMENT exits, eating strawberries.

LADY SCHWARZKOPF sings 'The Ash Grove' by Benjamin Britten.

LADY SCHWARZKOPF:

'Down yonder green valley where streamlets meander,

When twilight is fading, I pensively rove,

Or at the bright noontide in solitude wander

Amid the dark shades of the lonely ash grove.

'Twas there while the blackbird was joyfully singing,

I first met my dear one, the joy of my heart;

Around us for gladness the bluebells were ringing,

Ah! then little thought I how soon we should part.'

A 1940s model train begins to move. It is driven by a live rodent.

A large rock falls to the ground.

The audience hear a voice, it is THE SPECIAL DETACHMENT. It should be spoken in the style of Nazi Propaganda.

THE SPECIAL DETACHMENT: *(Voiceover.)* We have been overwhelmed by this special event.

The human mind will not function when it is hot. Only when it is cool and dispassionate.

If you are not careful you will no longer be human. If you are not careful you will become animals covered in sand. You are our descendants. You are very special.

JESSIE, the male twin awakes. He is very frightened. JESSIE takes his binoculars and looks to the sky.

Some of you are to be precisely registered and preserved. You will become our most important historical monument.

Beat.

Am I being clear?

Beat.

The future will look to you. We are very excited. We hope that you will be too. We are sure that you will be very pleased with the outcome. Another satisfied individual.

LADY SCHWARZKOPF: *(From 'Ode to St Cecilia' by Henry Purcell.)*
Soul of the world! Inspir'd by thee,
The jarring seeds of matter did agree.

THE SPECIAL DETACHMENT: *(Voiceover.)* Complacency is not an option.

Beat.

Am I being clear? Our fundamentals are clearly animal.

LADY SCHWARZKOPF: *(From 'Ode to St Cecilia' by Henry Purcell.)*
A quiet conscience, in a quiet breast,
Has only peace, has only rest.

THE SPECIAL DETACHMENT: *(Voiceover.)* We are, in fact, moving meat.

A stone falls to the ground.

JESSIE: We looked up, but nothing. Where were those friendly bombs to fall on us? Where was the world when you needed it most?

THE SPECIAL DETACHMENT: *(Voiceover.)* The great and terrible day has finally come.

JESSIE: For want of a nail the shoe was lost,
For want of a shoe the horse was lost.

Beat.

Oops. Gone again.

> *The model train driven by the live rodent moves along its tracks. JESSIE takes a stone from one of the linen bags. He places it gently, and carefully on to the pile of stones.*
>
> *He repeats the process.*
>
> *The train stops.*
>
> *LADY SCHWARZKOPF sings the first section of 'Death and the Maiden' by Franz Schubert.*

LADY SCHWARZKOPF:

Das Mädchen:

Vorüber! Ach, vorüber!

Geh, wilder Knochenmann!

Ich bin noch jung! Geh, lieber,

Und rühre mich nicht an.

Und rühre mich nicht an.

(The Maiden:

Pass me by! Oh, pass me by!

Go, fierce man of bones!

I am still young! Go, rather,

And do not touch me.

And do not touch me.)

> *The train stops.*
>
> *Pause.*
>
> *The train begins to move once again. JESSIE repeats the process with the stones.*

JESSIE: A kind gesture. In memoriam. We felt that the world had completely.

> *Beat.*

Sorry. Gone again. Disgusting.

> *LADY SCHWARZKOPF sings the second section of 'Death and the Maiden' by Franz Schubert.*

LADY SCHWARZKOPF:

Der Tod:

Gib deine Hand, du schön und zart Gebild!

Bin Freund, und komme nicht, zu strafen.

Sei gutes Muts! ich bin nicht wild,

Sollst sanft in meinen Armen schlafen!

(Death:

Give me your hand, you beautiful and tender form!

I am a friend, and come not to punish.

Be of good cheer! I am not fierce,

Softly shall you sleep in my arms!)

JESSIE: *(Placing another stone.)* They are for the dead. But we never seem to have enough.

> *LADY SCHWARZKOPF sings 'Hear my Prayer' by Henry Purcell.*

LADY SCHWARZKOPF:

'Hear my prayer, O LORD, and let my cry come unto thee'

> *A cheerful sunshine slowly appears through a frosty window.*

JESSIE: I am a seagull.

LADY SCHWARZKOPF: *('Hear my Prayer' by Henry Purcell.)*

'Hear my prayer, O LORD, and let my cry come unto thee'

> *Beat.*

JESSIE: No that's not it.

LADY SCHWARZKOPF: *('Hear my Prayer' by Henry Purcell.)*

'Hear my prayer, O LORD, and let my cry come unto thee'

Beat.

JESSIE: I killed a seagull. Yes. On a rock. Good. That's it. Is it? Oh my heart. I wanted to lay it at your feet. But I forgot.

Pause.

/ Is that it?

LADY SCHWARZKOPF: *('Hear my Prayer' by Henry Purcell.)*
'Hear my prayer, O LORD, and let my cry come unto thee'

LADY SCHWARZKOPF: *(From 'Ode to Cecilia' by Purcell.)*
Thou didst the scatter'd atoms bind,
Which by the laws of true proporton join'd,
Made up of various parts one perfect harmony.

JESSIE: You're still here then? Not gone? I had the feeling you were all toast?

> *The model train driven by the live rodent moves along its tracks. JESSIE takes a stone from one of the linen bags. He places it gently, and carefully on to the pile of stones.*

JESSIE: Two roads diverged in yellow woods. In pondering one? In pondering both?

Pause. The train stops.

JESSIE: It's gone. Sorry. Strange. I wish I could remember the correct line.

Beat.

THE SPECIAL DETACHMENT: *(Voiceover.)* Blau was the one I talked to the most. Him, and his wife.

JESSIE: The seagull was huge. Just lying there. Who would have thought it? / Poor creature.

LADY SCHWARZKOPF sings 'Lord, what is man?' By Henry Purcell, realised by Benjamin Britten.

LADY SCHWARZKOPF: Lord, what is man, lost man,
That Thou shouldst be so mindful of him?
That the Son of God forsook his glory, His abode,
To become a poor, tormented man!
The Deity was shrunk into a span,
And that for me, O wound'rous love, for me.

THE SPECIAL DETACHMENT: *(Voiceover.)* Blau was the one I talked to the most. Him, and his wife. There was a knock at my door. It was my friend Blau. He looked very worried. He said that his Father had arrived on the morning's transport and was there anything I could do to help.

 Beat.

THE SPECIAL DETACHMENT: *(Voiceover.)* Help? Really Blau. How can I help. Your father is eighty. Really son. It is simply impossible.

 Beat.

Later that afternoon he came back to my office, tears running down his face. He said that it was all over, and that he wanted to thank me.

JESSIE: An / act of kindness.

THE SPECIAL DETACHMENT: *(Voiceover.)* There was no need for him to thank me, but I said if he really, really wanted to, then he could. Only if he really wanted to.

 Pause.

THE SPECIAL DETACHMENT: *(Voiceover.)* A man of eighty? Please. There was absolutely nothing I could do to help. The decision was out of my hands.

JESSIE lights the candles on the Birthday cake.

JESSIE: Two roads diverged in yellow woods, in pondering one, I took the other.

JESSIE makes a farting noise with his mouth. Pause.

JESSIE: And that made all the difference.

Beat.

JESSIE: *(To BESSIE.)* It's been what seems like years.

JESSIE makes another farting noise with her mouth. He clenches his fist. He looks at it.

JESSIE: Pathetic.

Beat.

JESSIE: Did I eat my Birthday cake I wonder?

To BESSIE.

JESSIE: *(Addressing the audience.)* Or did you eat my Birthday cake?

JESSIE makes another farting noise with his mouth. He lights the candles on the cake.

JESSIE: *(To BESSIE.)* Why do I always end up having to do this on my own? Its nothing short of tragic.

JESSIE closes his eyes to make a wish.

JESSIE: Please God.

JESSIE blows the candles out.

THE SPECIAL DETACHMENT: *(Voiceover.)* When you create an environment that allows females to behave like animals you do realize quite quickly, that every female must be carefully examined before she is entitled to enjoy any measure of respect.

> *The model train driven by the live rodent moves along its tracks. JESSIE takes a stone from one of the linen bags. He places it gently, and carefully on to the pile of stones.*

LADY SCHWARZKOPF: *(From 'Lord, what is a man?')*
    The Deity was shrunk into a span,
    And that for me, O wound'rous love, for me.
    Lord, what is man, lost man,
    That Thou shouldst be so mindful of him?

JESSIE: *(To the audience.)* Once upon a time there was a beautiful Christmas tree.

LADY SCHWARZKOPF: *(From 'Lord what is a man?'.)*
    That the Son of God forsook his glory, His abode,
    To become a poor, tormented man!

JESSIE: *(To the audience.)* And under that Christmas tree was a mountain of presents. Present? In that place? I could not believe it. At roll call our names were called. We were all present and correct. Then the tree burst into light with a thousand candles.

LADY SCHWARZKOPF: *(From 'Lord, what is a man?'.)*
    Oh! for a voice like yours to sing
    That anthem here, which once you sung above.

JESSIE: We ran as fast as our teenie weenie little legs could carry us. What could our present be? The excitement was palpable.

LADY SCHWARZKOPF: *(From 'Lord, what is a man?'.)*
    Hallelujah.

JESSIE: Christmas? Who would have thought it. In that place.

> *JESSIE takes a carving knife out of the inside of his trousers. He points it at BESSIE.*
>
> *The following is taken from the Scottish folk tale 'The Cruel Mother.'*

JESSIE: *(Looking at the knife.)*
  'She pitched her back against a thorn,
  All alone and loney,
  And there she had her babies born.
  All down by the greenwood side.
  All alone and loney,

> *Beat.*

The memories are naturally difficult.

> *Beat. JESSIE looks at the present.*

JESSIE: *(Addressing the audience.)* I bet you are all dying to know what's in it?

> *Beat.*

JESSIE: Shall I put you out of your misery?

> *Beat.*

JESSIE: Only a little corner though. Just for you. Since you have been so good. But nobody else must ever know.

> *JESSIE opens a corner of the parcel, we can see linen printed with bright red strawberries.*
>
> *LADY SCHWARZKOPF sings 'Oh Sleep Why Dost Thou Leave Me' from 'Semele' by Handel.*

LADY SCHWARZKOPF: Oh sleep again deceive me.

> *BESSIE awakes with a scream.*

BESSIE: STRANGER DANGER!

LADY SCHWARZKOPF: 'Oh sleep again deceive me.'

BESSIE: / Remember me?

LADY SCHWARZKOPF: Oh sleep again deceive me.

BESSIE: Remember me Jessie? / REMEMBER ME?

LADY SCHWARZKOPF: Oh sleep again deceive me.

JESSIE: Nope. Sorry. Don't / think so.

BESSIE: I don't ring any bells?

JESSIE: Not today Josephine. / Not today.

LADY SCHWARZKOPF:
    Oh sleep, Oh sleep, why dost thou leave me,
    Oh sleep again deceive me.

>   *BESSIE screams.*

JESSIE: STRANGER DANGER!

>   *JESSIE hands BESSIE the unopened present.*

JESSIE: I did remember yesterday.

BESSIE: Oh no.

JESSIE: Oh yes.

BESSIE: Oh no.

JESSIE: Oh yes.

BESSIE: *(Scared.)* The present.

JESSIE: Mmmmmm.

BESSIE: No.

JESSIE: OPEN IT!

BESSIE: No.

JESSIE: Move forward.

BESSIE: All alone?

JESSIE: Pass the parcel / Bessie.

BESSIE: *(About the knife.)* That looks sharp.

JESSIE: I think it could / be sharper.

BESSIE: Gut a fish?

> *JESSIE says nothing.*

BESSIE: Skin a rabbit?

> *JESSIE says nothing.*

BESSIE: Open a broken heart?

> *Beat.*

JESSIE: *(From 'The Cruel Mother'.)*
    'She saw two babes a-playing at ball,
    All down by the greenwood side.
    One dressed in silk, and satin,
    All alone and loney,
    The other stark naked as ever was born.'

> *LADY SCHWARZKOPF, sings 'Two Daughters of*
> *this Aged Stream', from 'King Arthur' by Purcell.*

LADY SCHWARZKOPF:
    Two daughters of this aged stream are we,
    And both our sea-green locks have comb'd for ye.
    Come bathe with us an hour or two;

Come naked in, for we are so.
What danger from a naked foe?
Come bathe with us, come bathe, and share
What pleasures in the floods appear.
We'll beat the waters till they bound
And circle round, and circle round.

BESSIE: Do you / love me?

JESSIE: Present now. / Love later.

BESSIE: I need / to know.

JESSIE: Present now. / Love later.

BESSIE: You do love me?

JESSIE: Present now. / Love later.

JESSIE: The present?

BESSIE: Am I Sweet?

JESSIE: / Present?

BESSIE: I do really wish I / could kiss you.

JESSIE: I'm bored.

BESSIE: A wet kiss?

JESSIE: Bored / stiff.

BESSIE: A big wet, sloppy, kiss.

Beat.

BESSIE: Are you done with the love in my heart?

JESSIE says nothing.

BESSIE: You. My darling boy. You make me so happy.

> *LADY SCHWARZKOPF sings 'Now that the Sun Hath Veiled His Light'. From 'Dido and Aeneaes' by Henry Purcell.*

LADY SCHWARZKOPF:
Now that the Sun hath veil'd his Light,
And bid the World good Night;
To the soft Bed, my Body I dispose,
But where shall my Soul repose?
Dear God, even in Thy Arms, and can there be
Any so sweet Security!
Then to thy Rest, O my Soul! And singing, praise
The Mercy that prolongs thy Days.
Hallelujah!

> *A model train driven by the live rodent moves along its tracks. JESSIE takes a stone from one of the linen bags. He places it gently, and carefully on to the pile of stones.*

JESSIE: *(JESSIE hands BESSIE a stone.)* Your turn?

JESSIE: Not today?

BESSIE: No. / Not today.

JESSIE: Not yesterday / either.

BESSIE: / No.

JESSIE: Maybe tomorrow?

BESSIE: Maybe. / Smacked bottom?

JESSIE: Guilty?

BESSIE: Of / course.

JESSIE: Still the same?

BESSIE: Mummy fell.

> *Beat.*

JESSIE: Yes. And?

BESSIE: She might have grazed her knee?

> *Beat.*

JESSIE: You didn't have a plaster did you?

BESSIE: No. They wouldn't give / me one.

JESSIE: Excuses, excuses.

> *Beat.*

BESSIE: I just wanted to dance.

JESSIE: / Poor Mummy.

BESSIE: Not too much to ask is it?

> *BESSIE takes her shoe off.*

JESSIE: *(Addressing the audience.)* She had some of her toes removed. Poor creature

BESSIE: Ballet. Tap. / Modern.

JESSIE: *(Addressing the audience.)* Frostbite.

BESSIE: Ballroom. Is this a ballroom? / Where are we?

JESSIE: I don't know anything anymore.

BESSIE: It certainly looks like a ballroom. Maybe I could dance here?

> *BESSIE shows her foot. There is blood.*

JESSIE: Oh look, There are no toes left.

BESSIE: All I cared about was swimming / and dancing.

JESSIE: How do you really know if an animal feels pain?

BESSIE: But I had to give them up. / All gone away.

JESSIE: The greater the promise. The deeper the wound. Tragic.

> *THE SPECIAL DETACHMENT enters. He eats a strawberry.*

BESSIE: STRANGER DANGER!

THE SPECIAL DETACHMENT: If you knew how I felt. I am ready to kill.

BESSIE: STRANGER DANGER!

> *BESSIE attempts to stand, but falls.*

JESSIE: *(Whispering.)* Look Bessie. It's him. He shot the seagull. Destroyed it. No rhyme nor reason. Just to / pass the time.

> *Confusion.*

THE SPECIAL DETACHMENT: Try. Really try.

BESSIE: Try really try.

THE SPECIAL DETACHMENT: Think. Really think.

BESSIE: Think. Really think.

THE SPECIAL DETACHMENT: The guilty will now enter an unknown world.

> *Beat.*

THE SPECIAL DETACHMENT: But we must not do anything to frighten them. She never got emotional.

BESSIE: She / wasn't me.

THE SPECIAL DETACHMENT: It is a matter of survival. Always of survival. Always put a limit to your actions. She never got upset.

BESSIE: She / wasn't me.

THE SPECIAL DETACHMENT: She never got nervous.

BESSIE: / She wasn't me.

THE SPECIAL DETACHMENT: My Mother was very clean. While using a knife, my Father cut his finger. He dressed it with a white bandage. The next day he decided to hit me. He put me over his knee and really leathered me. My Mother watched. Smiling.

'Mother's Advice'.

THE SPECIAL DETACHMENT: Mother told me that I should,
Do my utmost to be good.
'Never kiss the boys,' said she.
So now I let the boys kiss me

I'm glad I took my mother's advice,
Mother's advice, mother's advice
'Never kiss the boys,' said she.
So now I let the boys kiss me

Pause. THE SPECIAL DETACHMENT is moved.

THE SPECIAL DETACHMENT: My Father thrashed me so hard, that the cut on his finger opened up, and blood poured out. I heard my Mother scream, 'Stop it. Stop it right now. You are splashing blood all over my lovely / new clean walls.

BESSIE: Well, wasn't that / just charming?

THE SPECIAL DETACHMENT: Failure should never be forgiven. The coldest earth was always my bed.

> *THE SPECIAL DETACHMENT exits. JESSIE is furious.*

BESSIE: What's that face for?

> *JESSIE says nothing.*

BESSIE: Are you in the huff?

> *JESSIE says nothing.*

BESSIE: *(Laughing.)* If the wind changes you will / stay like that.

JESSIE: It is always best to stick with the crowd. Best never to be on your own.

> *JESSIE takes the knife out.*
>
> *Pause.*

JESSIE: Happy?

BESSIE: What?

JESSIE: Are you happy?

BESSIE: Yes. You?

JESSIE: Oh, I don't know anymore.

BESSIE: Do you know what / happiness means?

JESSIE: No.

BESSIE: Disappointing.

> *Beat.*

JESSIE: I don't care anymore.

Beat.

BESSIE: You do look cold.

JESSIE says nothing.

BESSIE: Are you cold?

JESSIE says nothing.

BESSIE: Are you freezing?

JESSIE: Yes.

BESSIE: Oh dearie me. If you ask me, this situation is near enough bloody criminal. Do you think you might die?

JESSIE: Yes.

BESSIE: Oh dearie me. As a baby you often went blue.

JESSIE: How would / you know?

BESSIE: Oh dearie me. It was awful. You were / nearly purple

JESSIE: Are you sure?

BESSIE: The cold was good for / you.

JESSIE: *(Warns.)* I want dates. / Times. Facts.

BESSIE: I mean you nearly died once. It was genuinely heartbreaking.

LADY SCHWARZKOPF sings from Purcell's 'King Arthur'.

LADY SCHWARZKOPF: Thou doting fool forbear, forbear!
What dost thou mean by freezing here?

At Love's appearing, All the sky clearing,
The stormy winds their fury spare.
Winter subduing,
And Spring renewing,
My beams create a more glorious year.
Thou doting fool, forbear, forbear!
What dost thou mean by freezing here?

BESSIE: They told me you would never, ever be / warm again.

LADY SCHWARZKOPF: We chatter, chatter, chatter. We chatter, / chatter, chatter.

JESSIE: You're a liar.

LADY SCHWARZKOPF: We chatter, chatter, chatter. We chatter, / chatter, chatter.

BESSIE: You even like to stand outside in the / cold.

LADY SCHWARZKOPF: We chatter, chatter, chatter. We chatter, / chatter, chatter.

JESSIE: Liar / liar. Pants on fire.

BESSIE: You were such a funny little character.

Pause. JESSIE stares blankly.

JESSIE: *(From 'The Cruel Mother'.)*
She pitched her back against a thorn,
All alone and loney,
And there she had her baby boy.
She drew her fillet off her head,
All alone / and a loney

BESSIE: *(Hysterical.)* Oh here, I've got something to / tell you.

JESSIE: / Oh yes?

BESSIE: Yesterday.

JESSIE: Oh yes.

BESSIE: In my / head.

JESSIE: Oh yes.

BESSIE: I know I / shouldn't.

JESSIE: / Oh yes.

BESSIE: It made me so very happy /. Jessie?

JESSIE: Oh yes.

BESSIE: Guess / what?

JESSIE: Oh yes.

BESSIE: You locked all the / doors.

JESSIE: Oh yes.

BESSIE: Would you like to / hear it?

JESSIE: Oh yes.

BESSIE: The story that made / me happy.

JESSIE: Oh yes.

BESSIE: Just you / wait.

JESSIE: / Oh yes.

BESSIE: You stayed with me. In our bedroom. You didn't let anyone in. Not a soul. And you said you would always look after me. You were not going to answer the phone. You would not go down the stairs and listen to the radio. You just sat and stared at me. With love, and a warm heart.

BESSIE is insistent. Pause.

JESSIE: You're being strange.

BESSIE: No / I'm not.

JESSIE: You are. You are being really / strange.

BESSIE: I'm not / being strange.

JESSIE: Like you have lost your marbles.

BESSIE: Are you going to lock / the door.

JESSIE: Maybe you need / assistance.

BESSIE: ARE YOU GOING TO LOCK THE / DOOR?

JESSIE: Maybe. / If you tell the truth.

BESSIE: DO AS YOU'RE TOLD. PLAY THE GAME. / THIS IS NOT FAIR.

JESSIE: You see. I told you so. You are being really, really, strange.

JESSIE presents her fist to BESSIE. JESSIE nods her head.

BESSIE: That's better. Can I have my pants down later?

JESSIE: Oh yes.

BESSIE: A good / smacking?

JESSIE: You have been a very naughty / girl.

BESSIE: I have been a very naughty girl.

JESSIE: Would you like your hot water / bottle now?

BESSIE: Yes. Thank you. / Lovely.

JESSIE: We are going to take your clothes off now, and put you to beddie byes. I'm a good little boy, but you are a naughty, / naughty little girl.

BESSIE: Bessie is a naughty / little girl.

JESSIE: I will feel the studs of your baby grow on my cold back. We will go to bed. Together. In our matching bed clothes.

BESSIE: Oh Jessie. I gurgle at / the thought.

JESSIE: Gurgle?

BESSIE: Yes.

JESSIE: Whine?

BESSIE: Yes.

JESSIE: Scream?

BESSIE: Oh yes.

JESSIE: With pure hate?

> *Beat.*

JESSIE: Organs failing?

> *Beat.*

JESSIE: Die? Rot?

> *Beat.*

JESSIE: Skin peeling from the bone?

> *Beat.*

JESSIE: Putrefy.

> *There is a silence. Diamond dust falls to the stage. JESSIE and BESSIE look up.*

BESSIE: Is it not strange that it's not snowing?

> *Beat.*

BESSIE: Last year by this time. It was already snowing. Do you remember? It was very, very cold. About thirty / degrees of frost.

JESSIE: I don't / remember.

BESSIE: You don't?

JESSIE: / No.

BESSIE: Oh I remember. / Clear as day.

JESSIE: I remember nothing. Blank.

> *Beat.*

JESSIE: You know I can't remember Bessie.

> *Beat.*

JESSIE: There was no snow.

> *The train moves once more, driven by the live rodent.*
>
> *JESSIE places a stone on the stage, carefully and gently as before.*

BESSIE: *(Addressing the audience.)* We were lucky you see. We liked the cold. Especially Jessie, as he loved the cold. The Greeks and the Spanish were all dead in three months. Do you remember?

JESSIE: / I don't remember.

BESSIE: It was awful. Really ghastly.

> *JESSIE strokes BESSIE's cheek. Tender. LADY SCHWARZKOPF sings from 'Die Walküre' by Wagner.*

LADY SCHWARZKOPF:

SIEGLINDE:
Bist du Siegmund,
den ich hier sehe –
Sieglinde bin ich,
die dich ersehnt:
die eigne Schwester
gewannst du zu eins mit dem Schwert!

> *JESSIE continues to stroke BESSIE's cheek.*

JESSIE: That must feel really, really nice.

BESSIE: Oh yes.

JESSIE: Better?

BESSIE: Oh yes.

JESSIE: Much?

BESSIE: Oh yes.

JESSIE: Good / girl.

BESSIE: You're a very, very kind person.

JESSIE: Yes?

BESSIE: Yes.

> *Pause.*

JESSIE: Isn't this funny?

BESSIE: Very funny.

JESSIE: I mean it just gets / funnier.

BESSIE: Doesn't / it.

JESSIE: Funnier and funnier. Just / look at you.

BESSIE: *(Laughing.)* / Oh stop.

JESSIE: If you were really to think about it. The state of you.

> *JESSIE gets a mirror out.*

BESSIE: I think I might wet my teenie weenie little girl / panties?

JESSIE: Will they get soaking wet?

BESSIE: Most likely.

JESSIE: You're an absolute shambles.

> *JESSIE presents BESSIE with her image in the mirror.*

JESSIE: Look.

> *BESSIE looks in the mirror. The laughter stops.*

JESSIE: Not so funny now.

> *JESSIE grabs BESSIE's face. Brutal.*

JESSIE: *(Threatening.)* I think you should look closely in that mirror, and ask yourself, 'Am I a good person.'

BESSIE: You're / hurting me.

JESSIE: Look at yourself, long and hard.

JESSIE continues to hold BESSIE's face.

JESSIE: *(From 'The Cruel Mother'.)*
    She drew the fillet off her heard,
    All alone and loney,
    She bound the baby's hands and legs
    All by the greenwood side. She drew…

> *JESSIE cannot continue.*
>
> *Painful silence.*
>
> *JESSIE releases BESSIE's face.*

BESSIE: What time / is it?

JESSIE: Ah. Tricky one. I think it might be somewhere between three o'clock and four o'clock.

BESSIE: In the morning?

JESSIE: Possibly?

BESSIE: Ah. Well. That all makes perfect / sense.

JESSIE: All over?

BESSIE: Maybe. Be more specific.

JESSIE: No.

BESSIE: Right.

JESSIE: Would you like a clue?

BESSIE: Oh, / yes please.

JESSIE: It is that time when time dissolves / into the sky.

BESSIE: Ah. Right.

JESSIE: Helpful?

BESSIE: No.

Beat.

JESSIE: So you're awake then?

BESSIE: Yes.

JESSIE: Are you sure?

BESSIE: Yes I / am sure.

JESSIE: Not lying?

BESSIE: No.

JESSIE: Can I really trust / you?

BESSIE: You know / you can.

JESSIE: No. Not anymore.

> *JESSIE takes his binoculars and points them at BESSIE.*

JESSIE: *(With a raised voice.)* How are you?

BESSIE: *(Confused.)* / I am fine.

JESSIE: I AM LOOKING AT YOU NOW.

BESSIE: / Right.

JESSIE: Do you want to come up?

> *A model train driven by the live rodent moves along its tracks. JESSIE takes a stone from one of the linen bags. He places it gently, and carefully on to the pile of stones.*

BESSIE: THE GERBIL MUST / STOP!

JESSIE: I think it's a hamster.

BESSIE: Oh. Really?

JESSIE: STOP HAMSTER!

> *The train stops.*

BESSIE: Must be a hamster.

JESSIE: START HAMSTER!

> *The train does not move.*

BESSIE: Maybe it's not /a hamster.

JESSIE: Actually, it might even be a rat.

BESSIE: Christ.

JESSIE: Not come yet.

BESSIE: *(Looking at the rat.)* Is it alive?

> *Beat.*

BESSIE: Well I never. Do you not think that it's a great shame that Jesus isn't coming?

> *Long silence.*

Pain.

BESSIE: Jessie?

JESSIE: Yes?

BESSIE: What's next?

JESSIE: No idea.

BESSIE: You are joking?

JESSIE: Nope. / No idea.

BESSIE: Disaster.

Beat.

JESSIE: Wait.

BESSIE: Yes.

JESSIE: I remember now!

BESSIE: Oh that's / super.

JESSIE: You're a bull.

BESSIE: / No.

JESSIE: In a ring.

BESSIE: / Wrong.

JESSIE: Your horns killed a man.

BESSIE: / No.

JESSIE: Blood from the groin.

BESSIE: / Wrong.

JESSIE: And I am a seagull.

BESSIE: / Wrong, wrong, wrong, wrong.

JESSIE: I am a seagull.

BESSIE: Wrong again. WRONG.

JESSIE: What?

BESSIE: No. Wrong.

JESSIE: Are you / joking?

BESSIE: WRONG.

JESSIE: But yesterday / you...

BESSIE: WRONG!

JESSIE: Not a seagull then? Bessie?

> *Silence.*

JESSIE: You said you knew. You cannot leave me like this. / All alone in the world?

BESSIE: Well. I decided that I had to make a few difficult decisions.

> *Silence.*

JESSIE: *(Smirking.)* You're frightened aren't you?

> *Beat.*

JESSIE: Big scaredy cat. I can feel it in our bones.

> *There is a pause. Sadness.*

BESSIE: It's very, very warm today.

JESSIE: We could keep the windows / wide open.

JESSIE: Even now, there are no leaves on the trees.

BESSIE: / The Birch trees?

JESSIE: When I woke this morning I saw a flood of sunshine.

BESSIE: There must / be leaves.

JESSIE: All the spring sunshine. I felt so moved and happy.

> *The train moves once more, driven by the live rodent.*
>
> *JESSIE takes another stone out of her pocket and places it on to the stage.*
>
> *A stone falls to the ground.*

THE SPECIAL DETACHMENT: *(Voiceover.)* I played with the children. I used to dress them up, give them delicacies. But when they did not amuse me anymore, I became indifferent.

> *Pause.*

BESSIE: Oh dear.

JESSIE: / What?

BESSIE: It's time.

JESSIE: *(Excited.)* Are you very Frightened?

BESSIE: Yes. Is it all the same people?

> *Beat. JESSIE looks at the audience.*

JESSIE: *(Excited.)* Oh yes. There they all are.

> *BESSIE screams.*

JESSIE: We should start.

BESSIE: No. Please. / Five precious minutes.

JESSIE: They will ask for their / money back.

BESSIE: Same as usual then?

JESSIE: / You start.

BESSIE: Do you think they know?

JESSIE: What?

BESSIE: Something that we don't.

JESSIE: Paranoid?

BESSIE: Yes. / Very.

JESSIE: Moron. Paranoia self destroya!

BESSIE: *(Referring to the audience.)* They know everything and still / they come.

JESSIE: Yes.

BESSIE: It's absolutely disgusting.

> *BESSIE stares at the audience with contempt.*

BESSIE: I can't. I cannot look at these / same faces.

JESSIE: Oh yes you can. You must.

> *BESSIE says nothing.*

JESSIE: Do it. Now.

> *BESSIE says nothing.*

JESSIE: Or pay.

> *BESSIE is upset.*

JESSIE: NOW. DO IT NOW. YOU STUPID GIRL.

> *BESSIE does nothing.*

JESSIE: Nothing at all?

BESSIE: No.

JESSIE: Typical.

> *JESSIE raises his fist to punch BESSIE.*
>
> *Long silence. Fear.*
>
> *BESSIE cries.*
>
> *JESSIE lowers his fist.*
>
> *The following dialogue should be addressed to the audience.*

JESSIE: We have travelled the world.

> *Beat.*

JESSIE: We were mostly involved in circus shows... In...

> *Beat. JESSIE continues to cry.*

JESSIE: BESSIE!

BESSIE: I am so sorry, I am trying.

JESSIE: Try harder.

BESSIE and JESSIE: *(Addressing the audience.)* We were in hostile regimes.

> *Silence.*

JESSIE: Oh no.

BESSIE: Sorry.

JESSIE: Not again.

BESSIE: Sorry.

JESSIE: Nothing?

BESSIE: No.

> *Beat.*

JESSIE: *(Addressing the audience.)* I don't care either way.

> *Beat.*

JESSIE: HISTORY MUST NEVER, EVER REPEAT ITSELF.

> *Silence.*

> *JESSIE starts to sing. BESSIE has become hysterical.*

> *'Controlling twins.'*

JESSIE: Your warmth, your warmth,
  Is so deep,
  Your gaze,
  Beams a hole inside me

> *Pause.*

JESSIE: *(Whispering to JESSIE.)* I am not doing this on my own.

> *BESSIE sings, she is in bits.*

BESSIE: Controlling again
  Un-separated twins
  Controlling again

JESSIE and BESSIE: You've sucked
  All the breath out of me
  You'll squeeze
  All the life out of me

  Controlling again
  Unsupported twins
  Controlling again

JESSIE: *(Addressing the audience.)* ARE YOU ENJOYING
  YOURSELVES?

> *Pause.*

JESSIE: Can you feel your pulse.

BESSIE feels her pulse.

BESSIE: Of course not. Don't be stupid. I have been up all night boiling eggs.

Pause.

JESSIE: *(With conviction.)* Always give the bigger half to your sister.

BESSIE: Our mother taught us that.

Beat.

BESSIE: We are the fruits of your imagination.

JESSIE: *(To BESSIE.)* Wrapped in the fog of YOUR unknown.

BESSIE: *(Addressing the audience.)* We always go to bed / at the same time.

JESSIE: At times of my deepest depression. I wish we were separated.

BESSIE: Humans who are separated seem like monsters to me. How strange and inadequate every movement would be.

Beat.

BESSIE: To sleep by myself.

Beat.

BESSIE: To eat by myself.

Beat.

BESSIE: To walk by myself.

Beat.

BESSIE: It all seems very lonely to me. It is the nightmare of swarming indistinguishable sameness.

JESSIE: Die Zwei is / Zweifel.

BESSIE: Two is doubt.

JESSIE: Die Zwei is Zwillingsfrucht am Zweige, / Suss und bitter.

BESSIE: Two is the twin fruit on the twig, both sweet and bitter.

> *Pause.*

BESSIE: Loneliness is a big killer you know.

JESSIE: Eh?

BESSIE: I heard it on the radio. LONELINESS IS A KILLER.

JESSIE: Sometimes you feel more lonely when you are with / someone.

BESSIE: But having each other is enough.

> *JESSIE says nothing.*

BESSIE: Jessie?

> *JESSIE says nothing.*

BESSIE: It is enough Jessie. Please. It is enough. Say it is enough. / Enough to be with me?

JESSIE: Are we really the fruits of imagination, wrapped in the fog of the unknown?

BESSIE: You scare me.

JESSIE: You know when there is a thick fog in the morning Bessie?

BESSIE: Yes.

JESSIE: And then by some sort of small natural miracle it clears in a jiffy?

BESSIE: / Yes.

JESSIE: I think that's how I feel right now.

Pause. Sadness.

JESSIE: There was a lady. We asked her if she knew where Mummy was. 'Don't cry', she said. 'Don't cry little ones. They are burning your parents.'

Silence. Diamond dust falls.

BESSIE: Oh look. Is it snow?

JESSIE says nothing.

BESSIE: It's not is it?

JESSIE: I / don't know?

BESSIE: It looks like / snow.

BESSIE catches some of it in her hands.

JESSIE: *(Sad.)* No. It's not snow.

BESSIE: / Is it our Mother?

JESSIE: Oh here, just you wait till you hear this.

BESSIE: / Was the snow our Mummy?

JESSIE: It's my birthday.

BESSIE: What?

JESSIE: It's my / birthday.

BESSIE: No.

JESSIE: Super news, eh?

BESSIE: You're being / ridiculous.

JESSIE: Time for us all to celebrate.

BESSIE: / LIAR.

JESSIE: Sing me Happy Birthday.

BESSIE: No. / LIAR.

JESSIE: Sing it now.

BESSIE: Liar, liar, pants / on fire.

JESSIE: I want Happy Birthday now. NOW. / I want it now.

BESSIE: It's not your / birthday.

JESSIE: Oh yes / it is.

BESSIE: It is not.

JESSIE: I knew you would be suitably surprised.

   (Sings.)
   Happy Birthday to me.
   Happy Birthday / to me.

BESSIE: Stop / it.

JESSIE: Happy Birthday dear / meeeeeeeeeeeeeeee.

BESSIE: This is / torture.

JESSIE: Happy Birthday to me.

BESSIE: Why are you doing / this.

JESSIE: Do I get a cake now?

BESSIE: No.

JESSIE: / With thirteen candles.

BESSIE: You are not getting a cake. Stop it.

JESSIE: Sing Bessie. SING.

BESSIE: Thirteen?

> *Silence. There is a stand-off.*

BESSIE: *(Sings.)*
> Happy Birthday to YOU.
> Happy Birthday to YOU.

> *BESSIE stops singing.*

JESSIE: CAT GOT YOUR TONGUE?

BESSIE: You're not thirteen anyway.

> *JESSIE clenches both her fists. There is a stand-off.*

JESSIE: Are you the bull Jessie?

BESSIE: *(Indignant.)* Happy Birthday TO Jessie.
> Happy Birthday / to YOU.

JESSIE: Excellent. Good girl. Now. I would like a clown now.

BESSIE: / No.

JESSIE: Tied up like dogs.

BESSIE: / No.

JESSIE: Cakes, and balloons / and clowns.

BESSIE: Stop this.

JESSIE: Have you made up the goodie bags.

BESSIE: What / goodie bags?

JESSIE: For the people coming to my party.

BESSIE: Shut up / now.

JESSIE: We can't have people leaving empty handed. I WANT
GOODIE BAGS.

>*Beat.*

JESSIE: With pieces of cake wrapped in tinfoil.

>*Beat.*

JESSIE: Not too much to ask. Is it?

>*Pause. BESSIE and JESSIE look at each other.
>Pain.*

JESSIE: Nothing more to say?

BESSIE: Nope. Not on / that subject.

JESSIE: At least I am not a liar.

BESSIE: Awww, shut up.

JESSIE: It is better to lose somebody with the truth, than to keep
them with a lie.

>*Beat.*

JESSIE: You don't even look like me.

>*Pause.*

JESSIE: I do have my own birthday you know.

BESSIE: No.

JESSIE: Make up the goodie / bags.

BESSIE: THIS IS NOT ENTERTAINMENT. What must everybody be thinking.

JESSIE: They are probably bored. I know / I'm bored.

BESSIE: The past.

JESSIE: Bored stiff. You want / the past?

BESSIE: Yes. Good. Progress. Much better.

JESSIE: Much better than the future?

BESSIE: God yes. / Much.

JESSIE: Or I could go silent?

BESSIE: Oh no. / Not that.

JESSIE: So silence is worse / than the truth?

BESSIE: Yes. Much. Much worse.

> *The rodent drives, the model train moves once more.*
>
> *JESSIE places another stone on the stage, gently and carefully.*
>
> *There is a long silence.*

BESSIE: Keep talking.

JESSIE: Anything / at all?

BESSIE: Yes. / Anything.

JESSIE: Any subject?

BESSIE: Yes.

JESSIE: The Good Uncle?

BESSIE: Yes. / Super.

JESSIE: Joseph Mengele?

BESSIE: / What about him?

JESSIE: Did you like / him?

BESSIE: At the / beginning.

JESSIE: Why?

BESSIE: He was like a father figure to us.

JESSIE: Not to me. What about the injections?

BESSIE: / Awful.

JESSIE: And the x-rays?

BESSIE: / That's terrible.

JESSIE: Endlessly getting measured.

BESSIE: / Oh, that's terrible.

JESSIE: Other twins' blood?

BESSIE: Terrible.

JESSIE: One day.

BESSIE: The special / day?

JESSIE: We were given something / special.

BESSIE: Oh I do love this story.

JESSIE: No you don't.

BESSIE: Of course I do.

JESSIE: What / the…?

BESSIE: I like it for the / right reasons.

JESSIE: Do you remember / the headaches?

BESSIE: Terrible.

JESSIE: The high fevers.

BESSIE: Really / terrible.

JESSIE: Did you think it was worth it.

BESSIE: Oh yes.

JESSIE: Really?

BESSIE: We were going to have a tiny, tiny little baby!

> *Beat.*

BESSIE: Five fingers. Five toes. Do you remember how sweet he was?

THE SPECIAL DETACHMENT: *(Voiceover.)* Mothers used to think that disinfectant was bad for children. I remember I saw one woman that knew what was going to happen and she found the courage to have a little joke with her daughter. She even played with her daughter's doll. It was very amusing.

> *The model train, driven by the rodent moves once again.*

JESSIE places another stone on the stage, gently and carefully.

LADY SCHWARZKOPF sings from 'The Faerie Queene.'

LADY SCHWARZKOPF: *(From 'The Faerie Queene'.)*
For at that Berth another Babe she bore,
To week the mighty Ollyqhant, that wrought
Great wreake to many errant knights of yore,
And many hath to foule confusion brought.
These twinnes, men say, (A thing far passing thought)
Whiles in their mothers wombe enclosed they were,
Ere they into the lightsome world were brought,
In fleshly lust were mingled both yfere,
And in that monstrous wise did to the world appere.

There is a pause. Sadness.

BESSIE: I am terrified now.

JESSIE: Awww.

BESSIE: Hold my hand.

JESSIE takes BESSIE's hand.

BESSIE: You see that's all you need. / A hand to hold.

JESSIE: Would you like to kiss me now?

BESSIE: Oh yes. / How wonderful.

JESSIE: Well you can't.

BESSIE: / Oh.

JESSIE: Tell you what, as a treat. I will blow you one instead.

JESSIE blows BESSIE a kiss.

JESSIE: Super?

BESSIE: Really super.

JESSIE: Well be warned. Don't get used to it. We could be at the end of the tracks.

Beat.

JESSIE: Bessie?

BESSIE: Oh yes.

JESSIE: What is the terrible curse for the human race?

BESSIE: Wigs?

JESSIE: No.

BESSIE: Cats?

JESSIE: No.

BESSIE: Bleach?

JESSIE: Stop.

BESSIE: PANTS!

JESSIE: No.

BESSIE: NAUGHTY DOGS.

JESSIE: Consciousness. That is the curse of the human race.
Well. I have decided, that I don't think I am very afraid of consciousness. I have acquired the curse of consciousness.

JESSIE clenches her fist. He looks at it once more.

JESSIE: It really is pathetic.

JESSIE takes the knife out of her stockings.

JESSIE: Not going to say anything?

> *BESSIE says nothing.*
>
> *JESSIE takes the knife to the join between them.*

BESSIE: / What are you doing?

JESSIE: I have decided, that I don't think I am very afraid of consciousness. I have actually acquired the curse of consciousness.

BESSIE: / Stop this.

THE SPECIAL DETACHMENT: *(Voiceover.)* And the eyes of them both were opened, and they knew they were naked. And they sewed fig leaves together and made aprons. But who was to say we were naked.

JESSIE: God did NOT say we were naked.

BESSIE: Were / they naked?

JESSIE: Nobody knows if they were naked.

BESSIE: But what about the fig leaves.

JESSIE: Well God was lying you see.

> *JESSIE is still brandishing the knife. He takes the knife gently across his chest.*

JESSIE: *(From 'The Cruel Mother'.)*
  She drew a little knife both long and sharp,
  All alone and loney,
  She pierced the baby's innocent heart,
  All down by the greenwood side.
  She wiped the knife upon the grass,
  All alone and loney.

JESSIE: *(Tender.)* Awwww. Do you miss your sweet and tiny little baby?

Beat.

JESSIE: Take the knife Jessie.

BESSIE does nothing.

JESSIE: TAKE. THE. SHARP. KNIFE.

JESSIE forces the knife into BESSIE's hand.

BESSIE: We were going to be a family.

Many rocks fall from the sky.

THE SPECIAL DETACHMENT: *(Voiceover.)* I have been trying to explain to you. You never listen. NEVER. It is shameful. You have to compartmentalize your thinking.

More stones fall.

THE SPECIAL DETACHMENT: *(Voiceover.)* Just as a for example. If the 'Subject' was the Government.

More stones fall.

THE SPECIAL DETACHMENT: *(Voiceover.)* The 'Object' was the Jews.

More stones fall.

THE SPECIAL DETACHMENT: *(Voiceover.)* The 'Action' was the gassing.

More stones fall.

THE SPECIAL DETACHMENT: *(Voiceover.)* Then we could tell ourselves the fourth element, 'intent' or 'free will' if you want to call it that. IT WAS MISSING.

BESSIE is terrified. She holds the knife.

BESSIE: But we were going to have a little family.

JESSIE: No.

BESSIE: You were the daddy. And I was the / mummy.

JESSIE: But the baby was gone. The Christmas tree.

BESSIE: Was I not / the mummuy?

JESSIE: With all the lovely candles. After roll call we ran as fast as our little legs could carry us.

> *JESSIE hands BESSIE the unopened present.*

JESSIE: Bessie?

BESSIE: Mummy?

JESSIE: Ready?

BESSIE: Daddy?

JESSIE: Steady.

BESSIE: Tiny little / BABY!

JESSIE: GO, GO, GO!

> *BESSIE rips the present open with the knife. A linen dress covered in bright red strawberries falls to the ground.*

BESSIE: *(Cheerful.)* We were given Mummy for Christmas.

JESSIE: Dead. Wrapped in Christmas paper.

BESSIE: Mummy was wearing her favourite summer dress with bright red strawberries on it.

JESSIE: Did you give her a tiny kissy wissy?

BESSIE: Yes. But she was terribly cold.

Long silence.

JESSIE: *(Pressing the knife against BESSIE's chest.)*
They pierced the baby's innocent heart,
All down by the greenwood side,
They wiped the knife upon the grass,
All alone and lonely,
The more they wiped the blood ran fast.

The model train falls off its tracks.

Chaos.

BESSIE: *(Addressing the audience.)* You must not dream.

There is a loud explosion.

BESSIE: *(Addressing the audience.)* It is only important to learn how to endure things.

There is another loud explosion.

BESSIE: *(Addressing the audience.)* But when the world does not act like humans.

JESSIE empties the bags of stones on to the stage.

BESSIE dies.

THE SPECIAL DETACHMENT: *(Voiceover.)* Blau was waiting for me. He had tears in his eyes. He stood to attention and said, 'Mein Herr, I want to thank you. I gave my Father a meal. And then they took him for a shower. 'It is all over now.' Blau said to me. 'Thank you kind sir. You are a good man. Thank you sir, from the bottom of my heart.

Beat.

THE SPECIAL DETACHMENT: *(Voiceover.)* I said to that Jew, 'You have no need to thank me Blau, but of course if you want to thank me, I will allow it.'

JESSIE: / Is it broken?

SPECIAL DETACHMENT: *(Voiceover.)* Let me tell you something. It is very important. I was nothing more than a cog in a wheel. Spinning. A big machine. But the machine is broken.

JESSIE: / I can't fix it.

THE SPECIAL DETACHMENT: *(Voiceover.)* After, I was allowed to join an all male choir. We were treated very well by all the people we stayed with.

> *Confusion. BESSIE takes out his binoculars and looks to the sky.*

JESSIE: We wanted the bombs to fall. To fall on us. But the bombs never came. The world knew. But the bombs never came.

THE SPECIAL DETACHMENT: *(Voiceover.)* What nice air. Let me smell it a moment.

> *JESSIE breaks away from BESSIE. He takes a bag of stones. He gives a stone to each of the audience.*

JESSIE: For the dead?

> *LADY SCHWARZKOPF sings 'Let the Bright Seraphim', from 'Samson' by Handel.*

LADY SCHWARZKOPF:

Let the bright seraphim in burning row,
Their loud, uplifted angel trumpets blow.
Let the cherubic host, in tuneful choirs,
Touch their immortal harps with golden wires.

THE SPECIAL DETACHMENT: *(Voiceover.)* Everything human has its origins in human weakness

> *JESSIE turns to BESSIE.*

JESSIE: Sleeping?

Beat.

JESSIE: I suppose you must be very tired.

Silence. JESSIE shakes BESSIE.

Wake up. Silly billy.

JESSIE shakes BESSIE.

JESSIE: Please wake up.

JESSIE shakes BESSIE.

Nothing.

JESSIE lights the candles once more.

JESSIE: Look my little sweetheart. It's your favourite part.

BESSIE remains still and silent. She touches BESSIE's face.

My goodness. You're absolutely freezing. I will try and find you a cozy blanket. To keep you cozy warm.

JESSIE kisses BESSIE. Tender.

JESSIE: *(Stroking BESSIE's cheek.)* We never did have the same birthday. You silly girl. We played let's pretend, and we were kept alive. There was no rhyme nor reason…

JESSIE smiles.

JESSIE: They wanted to give us sweeties, but all we really wanted was a cuddle. Stupid.

Pause. She touches BESSIE's face.

Stone cold. Terrible.

JESSIE picks up the blanket and covers BESSIE with it.

JESSIE: *(Sings.)* Sleep, baby, sleep
Your father tends the sheep

Your mother shakes the dreamland tree
And from it fall sweet dreams for thee
Sleep, baby…

> *Pause. JESSIE looks at the audience.*

JESSIE: Gone again. I wish I could remember the rest of it.

> *JESSIE closes his eyes. He makes a wish.*

JESSIE: Please God.

> *JESSIE begins to usher the audience out.*

JESSIE: You must go now. All of you. Nobody wants to see this. I am angry with anybody. I do not wish anybody any evil. I am unable to do so. I do not know how one can do it. I am not here to be loved and admired, but to act and to love. It is not the duty of other people to help me, however, it is my duty to look after the world, and the people in it. / Forever let the memory of us all be a cry of despair to humanity.

> *The Blind Soprano sings 'When I am laid in earth' from 'Dido and Aeneas' by Henry Purcell*

LADY SCHWARZKOPF: *(Beside herself.)*

When I am laid, am laid in earth,
May my wrongs create
No trouble, no trouble in thy breast;

When I am laid, am laid in earth,
May my wrongs create
No trouble, n trouble in thy breast;

Remember me, remember me
But ah! Forget my fate

> *The Soprano lies flat down on her blanket. We see the blood on her back once more.*

LADY SCHWARZKOPF:

> Remember me,
>
> But ah! Forget my fate

> *As the audience exit they are faced with themselves.*
>
> *THE SPECIAL DETACHMENT enters on to the stage once more with the audience, he is wearing a non-specific uniform. THE SPECIAL DETACHMENT is feeding the audience strawberries.*
>
> *There is a loud explosion.*
>
> *The stage goes to black.*
>
> *There is a loud explosion.*
>
> *The stage goes dark.*
>
> *THE SPECIAL DETACHMENT exits, eating strawberries.*
>
> *LADY SCHWARZKOPF sings 'The Ash Grove' by Benjamin Britten.*

LADY SCHWARZKOPF:

> 'Down yonder green valley where streamlets meander,
> When twilight is fading, I pensively rove,
> Or at the bright noontide in solitude wander
> Amid the dark shades of the lonely ash grove.
> 'Twas there while the blackbird was joyfully singing,
> I first met my dear one, the joy of my heart;
> Around us for gladness the bluebells were ringing,
> Ah! Then little thought I how soon we should part.'

> *A 1940s model train begins to move. It is driven by a live rodent.*
>
> *A large rock falls to the ground.*
>
> *The 1940s model train set stops.*

> *The audience hear a voice, it is THE SPECIAL*
> *DETACHMENT. It should be spoken in the style*
> *of Nazi Propaganda.*

THE SPECIAL DETACHMENT: We have been overwhelmed by
this special event. You must not dream. It is only important to
learn how to endure things.

The human mind will not function when it is hot. Only when
it is cool and dispassionate.

> *Chaos.*
>
> *The world continues to spin and spin.*
>
> *Interminable.*
>
> *There is no END.*

OTHER RUSSELL BARR TITLES

Sisters Such Devoted Sisters
9781840025675

Vantastic / Lobster
9781840029802

A Dish of Tea With Dr Johnson
Adapted by Russell Barr, Ian Redford
& Max Stafford-Clark
9781849431064